DESTINATION
SUCCESS

The Official Guide on
How to Develop
Winning Marketing Strategies

Disclaimer

This publication is designed to provide accurate and authoritative information in regards to the subject matter covered. It is sold with the understanding that the author nor publisher are engaged in rendering any legal, accounting, or other professional services. If legal advice or other assistance is required, the services of a competent professional person should be sought.

From a Declaration of Principles jointly adopted by a Committee of the American Bar Association and a Committee of Publishers and Associations

DESTINATION SUCCESS

The Official Guide on How to Develop Winning Marketing Strategies

Chris A. Hawn

The Official Guide on How to Develop Winning Marketing Strategies

Contents

Contents

Acknowledgements

THIS BOOK couldn't have been written without the help of many people. First and foremost is my wife Terry who has always encouraged me to follow my passion and supported my ideas and dreams. All the words that relate to motivation, inspiration and encouragement have been focused in my direction from her and the patience she showed me when I didn't deserve any was phenomenal. My daughter Jamee who inspired me to set the bar high to accomplish one of my many goals. Part of writing this book was to show by example what you can do when you put your mind to it. At the young age of 22, she has traveled the world extensively and plans to continue her travels. It is my hopes that this book will inspire her to put her experiences to paper as well. My father Bernie who has passed away taught me to share and teach others what I know. I would be remiss if I did not acknowledge that his spirit continues to live within me and a big part of sharing these strategies is to teach so others can prosper from my experience and knowledge. And where would I have been without the sounding board of my sister in law Diane Rifkin. She always listened, gave feedback and was positive in every way. Her guidance was really felt and greatly appreciated.

After my family there is an amazing team of people who have helped me complete this project through their encouragement and support. Gerry Rose took me under his wing and shared with me many of his ideas and concepts years regarding network marketing. Gerry lives by many of the principals written about in this book. He stimulated my brain and opened my eyes to the possibilities of advancing a way of doing business. I consider Gerry a mentor and a friend. My second wife (as my wife Terry calls her) is Patty Vogan of Victory Coaching. For someone I was not actually married to, I received more support and encouragement as well as praise for my ideas than anyone I could imagine. Patty and I have similar minds in that we are always thinking about how to do things better, faster and more efficient. Her personal coaching over the years has kept me following this dream of writing a book. Her persistence to push me just by gently asking how the book is doing motivated me to bring it to a conclusion. I would also like to acknowledge one of my best friends, Norm "Neuman" Kaufman for the phone calls to pick me up and all his support over the years.

Last but not least I want to thank Leonard Szymczak for showing me the ropes of getting the book to print. Without Leonard's counsel, comments and feedback in the late innings, I'd probably still be writing. And without the help and support of the team at Ameriguard Communications, we'd have nothing. Thank you from the bottom of my heart.

To all of these people, I am eternally grateful.

Chapter 1

Introduction

L ET'S FACE IT. It's a jungle out there and everyone is trying to sell you something or get you to use their product or service. The jungle is full of dangerous animals and plants that can harm you, but within, there are also those that can help you stay alive.

Today's consumer is savvy, smart and skeptical. They want benefits and not just a pretty picture of what you are about. They are interested in what THEY are about and what you can do for them.

This book shows you the way to navigate through the jungle. Instead of finding a way through the trees and swampy areas, you will plan for a predictable and prosperous path through the business world and more specifically, your own community. As the highly respected Zig Ziglar would say, **"Get wired to be inspired".**

I grew up in a middle class family in Southern California. As a boy, I did the usual stuff most American boys do. Boy Scouts, Little League, bike riding and hanging out with my friends. I always wanted a paper route but it seemed like the "other "kids always got a route when one became available. So my pals and I had to get creative to be able to buy that candy bar or RC Cola at the local drug store. Back then you would get 3 cents for a returned bottle so we were always on the lookout for empty coke bottles to return.

Not far from my home there was what we called the "Forest". It was a grove of old Eucalyptus trees the railroad company had planted to be used to help supply railroad ties. We could hide, climb trees, make forts and have all kinds of fun and I loved it there. The interesting thing about this forest was that it ran alongside a golf course where one of the fairways ran parallel to the street along the forest edge. We had never paid close attention to that golf course until the day that the course management put up a fence dividing the edge of the fairway and the road that separated it from the forest.

One day we were playing at the edge of the forest and a golf ball came ripping over our heads and landed nearby on what I would soon call "our side of the fence". The golfer who hit that ball soon approached the side of the fence where his ball went out of bounds and yelled at us to get his ball. I fetched the ball, passed it through the chain linked fence to the golfer and he presented me with a quarter.

We soon realized that the golfers were unable to retrieve their golf balls after an errant drive which traveled over the fence but more importantly, we realized that these golfers would pay us to retrieve their golf balls. It wasn't long until we learned the value of a lost golf ball.

If the ball was new and unmarked, it was worth a quarter to us. If it had a little blemish on it from hitting the road, it was worth 15 cents and if it was in bad shape, we'd take a dime for it.

This was it. We had hit pay dirt. No getting up early to deliver papers. Heck, they could keep their paper routes. We figured out how to make money around the golf course while still having fun. Eventually we discovered that we could go into the ponds at night when the golfers and grounds keepers we not around and collect as many as 100 golf balls in a single night. We'd take them home, clean them up and then sell them through the fence the next day to the golfers for significantly less than what a new ball was costing them.

We learned the concept of a packaged deal by making bags of balls that we would sell in bulk. So this was my first experience in being an entrepreneur and a marketer as I kept finding new ways to collect and sell my golf balls.

Fast forward 12 years...... I earned my doctorate at Palmer College of Chiropractic in Davenport, Iowa. I came back to California to open my practice and since I was newly out of school and had no money I ended up renting space in another doctor's office in return for a percentage of my collections. It wasn't long before I was up and running.

I placed an ad in the local penneysaver and soon business was brisk and I developed a very successful and profitable practice in less than one year. There was no managed care, there were no insurance panels. It was an even playing field.

Not wanting to be under someone's wing, I now figured that I had the experience to get going and enough money to open my own practice and so that is what I did. I opened an office in Westminster California.

Soon thereafter managed health care hit and I didn't think I needed to participate. I was not about to have someone else tell me how to treat my patients so I plugged along occasionally losing a patient or two because I wasn't on their designated insurance panel.

I didn't see the writing on the wall because I was so busy. I couldn't imagine losing a good part of my patient base due to managed care. My early and easy successes blinded me to what was really happening. I didn't worry about competition or anything else for that matter.

Life was good. My main marketing revolved around athletes and sports. I had many professional athletes as patients including a few LA Lakers and Utah Jazz players. This cliental attracted others who wanted to go to the guy who treated the guy.

The time had come where I made the decision to relocate to a coastal town where I could start a family. This would mean selling the Westminster practice and starting all over again. I was young and made the decision that I could do this.

I moved to a beautiful city in Southern California where I met my wife and where I would spend the next 23 years.

After opening the new office, I began going to all the social events, chamber of commerce functions, and even joined the local Rotary Club. Instead of just randomly advertising like I had in the past I developed a strategy that comprised of a plan for continued contact with those I met. The initial strategies have been refined over the years and you will understand and own these strategies by reading this book.

Since initiating the marketing strategies over the past 20 years, the strategies have been added to and modified to fit today's technology. They are so effective that they can be applied to almost any small business.

When ethically and morally sound minds come together and pull their ideas together, you can count on something good happening. These ideas are not mine alone. What I can tell you is that I have studied over 106 marketers and gurus by spending thousands of dollars on books, interviews, DVDs. CDs, seminars, webinars, videos, tutorials, blogs, forums and whatever else is out there. I even took a job as a medical sales representative to get the companies coveted two week sales training course.

I've taken this knowledge of what is working now and put it on steroids by combining it with even more techniques to complete this marketing guide. So I can tell you without fail, I have taken the best of the best, combined it with the rest and brought you the official guide to building your business through building relationships and focusing on a very specific "target market" approach.

My entrepreneurial spirit kicked into high gear and I started two totally unrelated businesses that are still active today. There are both based on the strategies you are about to learn.

I have always loved marketing and Chiropractic. But you have to be smart to survive.

We really are in a jungle today and with all the internet technology dominating the marketplace you better be in the relationship game or like a lot of the other creatures in the jungle, you will be eaten. Follow the strategies and make your own path. There are no "one shot wonders" and you need staying power. This guide will show you how to do it.

My knowledge is based on 28 years as a health care provider and marketer. I have traveled the world and have seen how people advertise and market their wares and services in places like Tonga, Indonesia, Europe, Turkey, Australia, Southeast Asia, Mexico, South America and the place I like to call home, the USA.

Through my experiences in various cultures and the advanced technology, I have found that no matter where you go there is only one constant to successful marketing. It is all based around relationships.

Chapter 2

Breaking It Down

A LTHOUGH THERE ARE literally hundreds of ways to market a business or service, this book focuses down like a laser on what I like to call Success MAPS (Marketing-Advertising-Promotion- Strategy)

When followed, this systematic approach is guaranteed to help you build **"Business Relationships"** which will bring ongoing business for years to come so long as you continue to sow the garden and weed the weeds.

I have discovered the secrets that will set you free in marketing your business and enable you to nurture the relationships that will eventually be a major part of your success. And YES, writing a book is one of the secrets, and YES I will provide the resources to show you how easy and cheaply you can get this done utilizing some of today's technology.

There are eight major strategies that you are going to focus on.

The Defining Statement

The first strategy is going to be on defining who you are and what business, service or product you have. You will develop a defining statement so everyone knows what you do and what you are about. This is fundamental in all the other strategies that follow and is the most important.

Communication Strategy

Your website, email, business card and social network profile all need to be in sync. You will learn the number one thing that all websites need to have, the type of email address you must have and what the appearance of your business card should look like.

Advocate Strategy

This involves the people who hold a special position in your networking pool. You will learn how to stay in present time consciousness with them while at the same time, not impose or exploit the relationship.

Correspondent Strategy

You will develop a system that allows you to keep in touch with a larger number of people. These people will come to expect to hear from you through a common, but refined way of staying in touch.

Networking Strategy

Instead of just meeting and talking to everyone, you will learn to develop a plan for any networking event. You'll learn who to spend time with, how much time and how to address each one. You'll take them to the next level to address what their needs are so you can find a way for your business or service to satisfy those needs. These will be the keys to making networking meetings successful while not wasting your time. When you have a plan, you increase your successes.

Presentation Strategy

You will learn how to you acquire speaking engagements with a few simple techniques. You will read about where to go to acquire special skills and learn how to overcome any difficulties you may have. You will become an effective speaker. There's a trick that could have you giving talks as often as 2 – 3 times per month.

Website Maintenance

SEO, function and new technology. You will only address this periodically but when you do, along with any other web 2.0 technologies that have come into play, you will update everything. This strategy is a bit like changing the oil in the car. Every 3500 miles you need to see what needs to be changed or updated.

Expos and Special Events Strategy

Schedule them and make them work for you. You'll develop a plan and call to action to create that reason to stay in touch. You'll see examples of what to do and how to do it.

This book was meant to be short for the fact that I want you to use it as a guide. Read it, re-read it and then read it again. Keep a notepad next to you because amazing and productive thoughts will come to you and you will want to remember them. If you don't write it down, it will get lost (in your mind or some other obscure place)

Highlight special parts in this book that stimulate your thought processes. Remember, this is a guide, not a novel. Go get that paper or highlighter right now. I'll wait.

Oh and by the way. I need to tell you that the names of individuals and businesses used in this book are fictional and are in no way associated with any language, affiliation, association or connection with the author or publisher.

Chapter 3

Sell Yourself as the Expert

O NE OF THE most critical things to address before even thinking about the rest is actually identifying who you are and what product you sell or what service you provide.

The Success MAPS system explains what a defining statement is, why it is essential to your success and then how to create your own defining statement that tells people who you are and what you do.

Before completing the Success MAPS system, you need to learn and understand how to present yourself as the expert in your field. You might be straining to figure out what kind of expert you are as you read this but I can assure you that you are an expert in more things than you can imagine. You are going to learn how to use your defining statement to attract the right clients or customers and generate more business and referrals.

The implementation of the first of the Eight Steps is the foundation of this book and once you have begun to put the action steps into play towards utilizing your Defining Statement, you'll be off and running. Your results will be directly proportionate to the effort you put in to it. But you will get results. I guarantee it.

Programming success habits into your life increases the odds of your success. This repetitive programming may take days, weeks or even months. It all depends on what you're doing, why you're doing it, who you're doing it for and most importantly, if you believe in what you're doing.

People are different and situations are different. I don't profess to know exactly what the exact amount of time each individual will take to program their habits. All I can say is that most people won't do what it takes to make these changes. Contrary to that I can say that I have personally found success in 30 days and I think this is a reasonable amount of time to expect to see the results. We track this with what we call our Scoreboard Strategy. I'll come back to this in a later chapter.

Lastly, at various places within the book you will find tips, techniques and resources to enhance your marketing even further.

There are literally hundreds of ways to market and advertise. No one knows everything and technology is constantly changing. Take a look at www.rbraintrust.com to see what is working currently on the internet and get some free tips.

This is a system that has been working time and time again because aside from it working for me, professional high priced consultants and coaches have been teaching this to business owners and company executives and charging as much as $5,000. Now you get all the secrets and more for the price of the book.

What you don't get is that $5000 X factor where an outside consultant guides you through the hurdles and barriers you will encounter. I have hired various consultants for periods ranging from one day to as long as one year. All I can say is that when I did EVERYTHING that I was being taught, I got the results and it was worth the money I paid. But let's not kid each other. It is difficult to stay on track and spend the big bucks.

The knowledge I have obtained and paid thousands of dollars to get is now only going to cost you a fraction of the cost. Basically, it is the cost of this book. What a deal!

Are you ready to get started?

Chapter 4

Strategy Overview

Fine Tuning the Engine

First, ask yourself

1. What is your current marketing strategy? Do you have one?

2. What activities are you currently employing to get clients, customers or patients?

3. Do you have a referral system in place?

4. Market via the Internet?

5. What kind of advertising do you do?

6. Do you have a website?
    - How do people find your website?
    - Does it offer a "Call to Action?"

7. Do you employ Social Networking"

8. Do you use video?

Make a complete list of what you are doing now and what it is costing you on a monthly basis. Go ahead, write directly into the book.

Current Marketing Activities: **Monthly Cost**

_____   _____

_____   _____

_____   _____

Stop reading! Go do this now before going on to the next step.

STOP !

Seriously....don't move on until you do this!

Welcome back.

When you are done making your list, ask yourself the following questions:

✦ Do I go to network meetings such as Chamber of Commerce, Rotary, Kiwanis, Leads Clubs, Le-Tip, Provisors, BNI, etc

✦ Do I market on the Internet?

✦ Do I have a referral system in place?

✦ Is the advertising I'm doing paying off?

✦ Do I have a website?

 ø How do people find my website?

 ø Do I offer a "Call to Action?"

 ø If so, how many take me up on that?

 ø How many of those do I convert to clients, customers or patients?

Now be honest with yourself.

How are these working for you?

Make a mental note of these answers as you will want to refer back to the things you are currently doing when learning the Success MAPS and how to use them more effectively. You are going to kick ass with what you are about to learn.

Describe your **"Ideal Client"**, customer or patient. Describe them in great detail and take into consideration goodwill, fashion, time of day you see them, time spent with them, money made by associating with them, their looks or anything else that stands out in your mind.

_____

_____

_____

Here's how this works. Review the diagram on the next page or download a copy you can write on at the following address: www.rbraintrust.com/ds/successmaps.com

Client Name:	Immediate Action	Every 30 days	Every 6 Months	Tools for Top Dogs	Secret Weapons
Client Task	**Defining Statement**	**Advocate**	**Website Evaluation**	**Webinars**	**Competition Killer**
• Make a list of 50 things and describe your product or service • Use 25 words or less to come up with what you do	• Review, rehearse and commit to memory • How do you do it? **Communication** • Evaluate your website • Call to action? • Email and domain name in sync? • Business cards • Social network profiles	• List of 25 **Correspondent** • Who you know **Networking/Events** • What, where and when **Presentations** • Make 100 calls • Give 1st presentation	• Improve function • Clean up links • SEO **Expos = Special Events** • Open house • Trade show • Booth Exhibit • Other event	• Weekly • Interviews **Video and Articles** • To enhance blog • Drive content **Blog** • Drive content	• Facebook advertising • Facebook fan page • G-mail advertising • Google Adwords • Craigslist

Chapter 5

Create Your System

YOU ARE GOING to create a system where you will begin doing two things immediately. There will be four things that you will do every 30 days, and there will be two things that you will do every 6 months (now and six months from now).

You're going to take what we call your **"knowns"** and **increase** those. You are also going review your **passive marketing** and put a **"proactive approach"** to it. As you increase your **knowns** and take a **proactive approach** to your passive marketing, you will get more clients/customers and more referrals. It's that simple.

"Knowns" = People you know and refer to you and support you as well as activities that already bring you business

"Passive Marketing" = Existing marketing and advertising that just sits in one place or has not proven to be cost effective

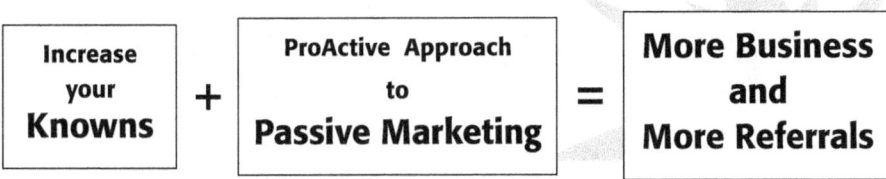

Simply by putting things in place and taking action on them you will get, a 20 – 80 % return on your time and energy. (Success Rate)

What this system will do for you is attract more customers and generate more referrals. The way this will work is with our 8 Step Success MAPS (Marketing–Advertising-Promotion-Strategy)

Chapter 6

The Defining Statement

A s you can see from the Success MAPS spreadsheet, one of the first things to take action on is the defining statement. If you haven't downloaded it yet, go to chapter 4 and review this.

The Defining Statement (some like to call it an elevator speech)

The defining statement has everything to do with being able to respond, reply and project a precise, concise and accurate answer to a question. And this question gets asked everywhere. This is a question you get asked at conferences, by friends, colleagues, or at a party by a complete stranger. Are you ready? Here it is.

What do you do?

If you can answer this in 10 seconds or less then this may just be a review for you and I congratulate you! But if not, follow along while you develop how you are going to answer when others ask you... what do you do? This is a process, not a slam dunk.

You've only got a few seconds, 20 at most to answer that question when people ask it. You'll answer this question many times as you actually hand out business cards, everywhere from networking events to social gatherings, and even when you're just going about the business of living and meeting new people.

This is one of the most powerful reasons to create a short, powerful mini-speech about your business. It's short, to the point, and explains what you do. And it is designed to get the individual to ask the second question which allows you the opportunity to actually tell them what you do.

A FEW TIPS:

Create **interest – don't go for the kill.** The goal isn't to make an immediate sale. It's to create interest by showing the benefit of what you do, the needs you can meet and the problems you solve.

Commit it to memory – but don't deliver it like a robot. Write it out and review it often. Practice it out loud until it flows naturally. Really connect with the benefit you provide, and how your customer's businesses and lives can be positively impacted by what you can do for them. Paste this up on your bathroom mirror so that you can rehearse it every morning. You must own it.

Give it often – it'll grow on you. The more frequently you deliver your defining statement, the more a part of you it will become. It will probably change over time, and in the beginning it's a great idea to create a few different defining statements to see which one feels most natural and gets the best results.

SOME SAMPLES:

1. I design and develop targeted marketing strategies to help businesses dominate their market.

2. I blend my two passions of Spiritual and Personal growth as well as writing into my career as a therapist and writer. I inspire and empower clients to be heroes in their personal novels and I help writers use psychological processes that connect them with the heart and soul.

3. I help make Google fall in love with people's websites so they can potentially double or triple their business.

4. I work with people who want to attract the right prospects and generate more referrals.

ACTION STEPS TO CREATING YOUR OWN DEFINING STATEMENT

Come up with a list of 50 ways and things that your business does to "answer the question," what do you do? You answer this question 50 times in 50 different ways.

Here are just a few samples of what a client of mine came up with: She specializes in recruitment of attorneys for large firms. This attorney sent me her statements answering the question, "What do you do?"

Upon receiving her response:

1. I then went through and <u>underlined</u> the outcomes the attorney's clients received.

2. I also highlighted their target markets.

What do I do? Defining statement

1. <u>Partner</u> with clients and candidates

2. Facilitate the recruiting process

3. Thoroughly <u>screen</u> candidates

4. Get to know the particular needs of clients and candidates

5. <u>Perform customized searches</u>

6. Work with trusted affiliates to fulfill various needs nationally

7. Provide <u>advice</u> and <u>counsel</u> to attorneys and law firms

8. Guide clients through the placement process

9. <u>Design</u> and <u>implement</u> a <u>strategic plan</u> for each candidate

10. Represent attorneys, law firms and companies

11. Work with law firms and companies to fulfill their attorney employment needs

12. Follow-up <u>to promote seamless integration</u>

13. All inquiries and <u>placements</u> are handled with the <u>utmost confidentiality</u>

14. Consult with firms regarding their marketing and support, as it relates to candidates

15. Provide interviewing expertise

16. Offer excellent testimonials and references

17. Offer a current website that clearly discusses the breadth of our business and services

18. We are active <u>participants</u> in each <u>placement</u> participate in placement

Now you will come up with two results that are typically 3 - 5 words in length. Plus you wanted to make sure they contain 1 – 2 keywords words relative to your target market that can be considered and adopted to be included with your 'Defining Statement"

After you complete the above analysis, spend some time playing with the words and make some observations:

Here are our observations in the example above:

Based on the entire list of 50 provided by our client, the client likes the words **"success, results, reliable, and value."**

We analyzed this list and found common words or phrases like **"work with"** and **"want"** or **"do you know how."** And these words and phrases are now used in one of our defining statements.

Using the Thesaurus and Dictionary can help find substitute words that are used less often, are shorter, and still remain on a basic language level. Work with these words to add to the experience and development, and then share the findings with a friend, family member or colleague for their response.

Review this example of the Defining Statement that the recruiter came up with.

"I work with clients who want to work with top attorneys and prospects who want to work for the best firms."

Something that you would ask yourself would be:

+ Do I have two target markets in my defining statement?
    One being 'clients' the other being 'prospects.'

+ How might you change the two results?

 # 1   Hire top attorneys and # 2, work for the best firms.

Ask yourself if you have any other thoughts on how to alter this to make it a basic language level, easily repeatable, and something you would like to say in representing yourself?

Get the other person who previously critiqued you to offer a new response. Use your gut instinct and go from there. This Defining Statement will become a huge part about what you do and say in the business world from here on out.

You must review, rehearse, commit and own your defining statement. You should not hesitate when saying it. But remember, don't say it like you are rehearsing something. Say it like you are speaking it. Calm, cool, and collected. This takes practice.

Now that you handled answering the big question. What do you do? Let's move to the next big question.

How do you do that? (this is in response to the first question "what do you do?")

Let's work on this response next. Remember, this is the question we are looking for. Our defining statement is supposed to stir up curiosity or a more in depth questioning by the potential client or customer. They're giving you an opening to tell them what you do and how you can help them.

Defining Statement
- Review, rehearse, commit and own
- How do you do it?

ACTION: I want you to say your Defining Statement 100 times/3 times per day/for 7 days. No excuses. Go strong or go home!

Side note: Past clients have stated that using a digital recorder to just constantly ask yourself the defining question, and then answering it has proved to be extremely helpful. While you are driving or sitting at your desk, ask yourself. What do you do? Answer and then repeat.

Congratulations!

You're on your way.

Chapter 7

Communication Strategy
.....what to say

THE NEXT STEP is to evaluate and improve (if needed) on the communication tools you already have in place. These tools are not limited to the following three items, but for the purpose of getting a jump start, these have to be right.

Website/Blog

It's quite easy and inexpensive to get a website nowadays.

You **must** have a website and or blog. Not only does it show that you are current with technology, but not having one shows that your business is really NOT in the game to win. I am going to assume that you have your own domain at the very least. If you do not have your own domain name you can go to godaddy.com or many other vendors out there and they will register a domain name for you. You need to get own your own name if it is still available. Yourname.com

This book is not about getting domains or about making a website/ blog as there are hundreds of books and websites out there to get you on your way. But you will need one so if you don't already have one, take the action steps necessary to get this done. Put it at the top of your list and do whatever it takes to get this done. It's easy and a no brainer!

The website/blogsite ties in with your personal and professional email addresses so that your customers know you are serious about your business.

Email

Think about it. Do you really think that an individual person doing business and using an email such as bob@gmail.com, bob@yahoo. com, or bob@aol.com exemplifies a professional business name? Get a domain, have an identifying email address to that domain and do it now. Do it today.

A sample of something that looks professional and will identify you with a business is bob@yourBusinessName.com. Get your domain name and a free email always comes with it. Try godaddy.com. They are reliable but certainly not the only ones out there.

When you send an email, have your defining statement and/or logo in the signature. That way your client will indentify you and connect you to your defining statement.

Business Cards

Have a professional business card made. Pass them out and promote yourself at every opportunity. After all, you picked up this book to get busy in business so let's do the basics. A business card that speaks about who you are is tool number I.

If you feel it is going to take some time to get it exactly the way you want it I suggest you go to www.vistaprint.com and get their free offer for some temporary cards. YOU MUST HAVE A CARD.

Design the fancy card later. Just get started with something right away. Fire now, aim later!

FIRE - READY - AIM

Pull out the Success MAPS spreadsheet again because that is where we are going to dig into now.

The following strategies are ones that need to be revisited every 30 days in order to keep continuity and complete your goal. The strategies are as follows:

+ Advocate

+ Correspondence

+ Networking/Event

+ Speaking/Presentations

Let's get started

Chapter 8
ADVOCATE STRATEGY

Finding your team

ADVOCATES ARE PEOPLE that bring the world to you. Or they can be trained to send business to you. An example of an advocate is someone that also makes connections. They are what we call "**Connectors**".

Incorrect:

I met you and I want to introduce you to a (contractor/patient/sales rep, etc) that I know who is looking for some work. I say....here is this person's business card, give him or her a call.

That is <u>not</u> a **connector**.

A **connector** is somebody that acts like this. "Ok Jim, let me make sure I have your information correct such as your phone number, email and the basic idea of what you can do or what you are looking for. I am going to call Joe and let him know that you are going to be calling him. I'm also going to follow up with you in five days. Is that OK? I'd like to be sure you were able to make the connection.

That's what an advocate is....and that is an example of a great one.

With this strategy, every 30 days you will send something of value. An advocate group of 25 people is a good number to start. If you have more and can manage more, fine. If you don't have 25, don't worry. You soon will. Advocates are people who do cross-referrals such as roofing contractors who might have the ability to refer the HVAC guys and vice versa.

Something of value.

Let's say you have written a book or a series of articles. Here's what you do.

Article

Let's say you're writing an article on "The 5 critical things you need to know before you trim a tree"! Send it to them as a courtesy FYI.

Book

You let your advocates know that you are writing a book and will be sending them a chapter of it, or a pre-release in February. If you choose to, you could send them a chapter a month before it's released or completed as a finished product. You can also notify them ahead of time to let them know that you will be doing this.

It allows you to make contact with them twice. In the first month you'll let them know what you're doing by saying something in an email like this. **"Here are the chapter titles I'll be sending you. Be on the lookout".** Tell your connector that you want them to have one of the first copies of this book when it is complete. Then, when it's complete send them a copy.

What it also does is that it creates some curiosity and excitement about you and what's to come. They know you and know what you are about. It reminds them that you are still out there and continuing to do your thing.

More examples of things of value

Here's something unusual...Most people send cards out at Christmas time. You can send cards out at times like St Patrick's Day with shamrock garland in it to bulk up the envelope. It now gets lumpy and will draw attention.

You can send Easter, 4th of July, Valentine's Day, or even Happy Spring (put a spring in the envelope to make it a lumpy card). How about this one….Happy Non Seasonal Greetings: With that one you might want to include a letter inside saying something like. "Just because it's September, it does not mean your ???. (I'll leave that to your imagination.) If you really want to do something great you can set up an account at smilebox. com or animoto.com and send animated cards reflecting photos of a trip you just took or something related to your connectors business.

Go to Marshalls, Target, Costco, the Dollar Store or Wal-Mart and find a box of 25 cards. Take them home and use your printer to ADD SOMETHING like your defining statement or something else that relates to the reason you are giving it to them and also make sure you personalize each one with something in your own handwriting.

E.g. It was great running in to you at the store and meeting your wife. Now I know Rebecca by name and I look forward to seeing the two of you again in the future. People need to know that you are not just doing a mass mailer. You always want to be sure to let these people know that they are something special to you.

Ninety per cent of the body of the letter can be made as the Hub (aka canned) template but it is what you do with that 10% of the greeting and closing of the letter that's going to make a difference over time. And make sure that you always include your defining statement in whatever you send out.

When you send mail, have your defining statement or logo on the outside of the envelope. Then, you must HAND ADDRESS each one of those envelopes yourself. This is not only going to work for you due to the law of attraction, but that unknown, misunderstood and undefined mental transference between you and that person will occur. And this is what you are after. Some call it Karma!

You might even have the argument that it works better because of "Less Touches and Less Personalization". In today's business environment, all the e-commerce and electronic applications have taken away a big part of how we personalize. A real card with a and written personalized message in it will go a long way.

Advocates are the people that are going to make your phone ring off the hook. Many years ago a colleague of mine shared a story of a business partner who did a presentation **called "How to make your phone ring off the hook"** He started these talks with this very same Advocate Strategy.

Sending these types of cards every 30 days is a good example of our Advocate strategy. Pick your holidays and plan ahead the exact date and the item or card that you will send in the non holiday times. If you write it down, it will get done. You must plan for this.

It is important to note that events you become aware of such as special occasions birthdays, deaths, sickness and celebrations are also an excellent time to connect. If not the marketing aspect, think about the human connection you can make.

Action Item 1 Identify and make a list of 25 people who you believe are your connectors.

Action item 2 Consider what your first offer will be. Maybe something tied to your Defining Statement

Send a personal Email to these folks and ask if you can communicate with them.

Your email would say:

E.g.

1st sentence: The reason for this email is to remind you and let you know that I work with

- women who want to take 10 years off their appearance by learning three simple tricks

- businesses to design and develop targeted marketing strategies to enable them to dominate their market

+ homeowners who want to save on energy costs and take full advantage of all the energy tax incentives while they last

+ people and businesses that want to attract the right prospects and generate more referrals.(my defining statement)

2nd sentence: Can I periodically send you information that has to do with attracting the right prospects for your type of business? (Related to your Defining statement)

Estimated positive response rate= 25 – 50%

For the person that does not respond. Email them again and ask them if they received the first email requesting permission to send periodic information. Recap what the first email said so they know what you are talking about.

If they say "NO" to giving you permission to send something, don't take that as a No to you. Only a No to wanting to receive more uninvited emails to clog their box.

Kill them with kindness and say "Ok, thanks for listening and (here is the key) let me know if there is anything I could do for you. Say it with a Smile and be Positive! I believe that in time, it will come back to you.

Chapter 9

Correspondence Strategy

Telling your story with articles

THIS IS WHERE YOU write an article every 30 days and then you email or snail-mail it to your defined list. These are NOT your advocates. They are everyone else that fits our criteria as being "Qualified".

In this instance the term qualified as it refers to a list, is a group of people who are qualified by being someone who meets one of the following objectives:

+ Send Business to you

+ Be Business to you

+ Have been business in the past aka past clients

Each article is 500 - 700 words and always has your bio, defining statement and contact information attached.

A newsletter does not satisfy this.

Part of what this is all about is keeping existing and potential clients engaged. You may send people your articles for months and even years and never hear from them. But then, all of a sudden you send them an article that hits home with "what they actually need" or they may have started a new business or know someone who has the ability to make an introduction. They may think of one of your articles when learning about the needs of a friend or colleague.

At 44 cents for a first class stamp, your total cost would be $5.28 per year plus the cost of paper. How are you going to beat that? Unless it is sent via email. I'm sure the value of just one of your products, services or commissions would far exceed this many years worth.

This strategy cannot be looked at like it is going to produce something big overnight. You are planting the corn as a seed. You don't pick the ears off it the day after you plant. Nurture it and let it grow.

You'll be surprised at how many people will contact you or comment on your article the next time you run into them. It's really effective if you write interesting content filled articles that connect with current topics and focus in a particular niche.

Don't get flustered and think you won't be able to write an article. Remember, you are an expert on many things. Just write about your topic and what is happening in your industry. Just as you would while posting in a blog.

Remember the digital recorder I mentioned in the chapter on finding your Defining Statement? This recorder can record your thoughts on a topic and all you have to do is put it to paper.

Asking questions is the best way to get material. Here is an example of writing an article about tree trimming.

Tree Trimmer: Hi my name is Peter and I own Peter's Tree Trimming service. Glad to meet you.

Interviewer: Peter, What is the most common question people ask you when talking to you about your services?

Tree Trimmer: Does it matter what time of year you trim a tree?

Interviewer: What is the first thing someone should ask when hiring a tree trimmer?

Tree Trimmer: Do you trim the tops of trees?

Interviewer: Why do you ask that?"

Tree Trimmer: I recommend that question because if they say yes, you have then identified a tree trimmer you DO NOT want to hire.

Interviewer: Why is that?

Tree Trimmer: It's the wrong thing to do because it puts too much pressure on the branches.

Interviewer; Then what else do you do?

Get the message here. Just think of a topic and then begin asking the questions and then answer them. There is your article. You could even interview some of your advocates or other people you know about their particular profession and as long as it fits into building business and others can identify with it, you'll be in great shape.

I can't resist telling you about a technique one of my clients (mortgage broker) used while building his website article database. He interviewed a targeted niche of people (Title, Escrow officers) who he knew did business with others and had a mailing list of their own clients (homebuyers, sellers and realtors). His article topic was tied into what the others business (title, escrow etc) was about and a topic he believed they would want their own customers or clients to know about. So, he did the interviews, wrote the articles based on the interview questions he asked and formatted a beautiful article.

He then sent each particular article to the person he interviewed in the form of a link via email for their review and approval. In the email he suggested to the business person that he send an email out to all their clients recommending that they read this article that was written based on an interview with him. He then directs them to the link that is attached to his email. You might have to explain to him how this works. Don't you think it sounds real flattering to the person that he was chosen to be interviewed and now you are suggesting that he sends this as a marketing tool to his clients?

All the better if you need to show them personally how to do this with a little TLC which will bond them to you even more. Remember, this is all about building relationships. In fact, you could even write an article about how to send articles to your client base. Brilliant!

Here is where you benefit again by doing this interview. Remember when I told you that each article is 500 - 700 words and always has your bio, defining statement and contact information attached.

Their clients will see your information as part of the article attached to the email. Here is the triple play

+ You get your article topic and content for creating an article for mailing or for your website

+ Your advocate or the person you have associated with and interviewed gets impressed with the fact that you want to interview them.

+ They also feel good because you have shown them a way to communicate with their clients and customers via their mailing list and their article.

+ You get exposure with your bio, defining statement and contact information that anyone reading the article will see.

On top of what I have shared with you right here. This can also be done with video which when combined with the tools available on the internet, can drive traffic to your site and increase your SEO.

ACTION ITEM 1

Create your first article of approximately 500 - 700 words utilizing your defining statement. To count the words in your article when you use Microsoft word, just highlight the text you want to count, then go to the "Tool Tab" and click on "Word Count". In windows 7, it is automatically displayed in the lower left hand corner of the screen. Don't forget to always have your contact information included with the article. So.….. every 30 days you must write an article utilizing your defining statement.

ACTION ITEM 2

Create distribution. Create a "one sheet" and use this as a tool to send out with whatever format you want. Personalize a note, and if snail mailing, hand print the envelope as stated previously. Make sure it is with an envelope that doesn't have to be folded. It may cost a bit more, but it will pay off in time.

Create a letter about who you have helped. Give them testimonials (with permission), Make a list of your clients, send them a picture related somehow to what you do or who you are...There are many things you can do

Ask them, what do you think of this?

If I was king of your world, what can I do for you?

SAMPLE: ONE PAGE

DESTINATION SUCCESS

The Official Guide on
How to Develop Winning Marketing Strategies
to Dominate your Market

Designing and develop your own personalized **Targeted Marketing Strategies**
utilizing our simple and easy to understand 8 step system.

**Discover how to create a Proven Systematic Marketing Strategy to allow you to
dominate your local market.**

- Master the simple concept of selling yourself as the expert
- Understand why developing a defining statement is critical
- Proven strategies for connecting with contacts without them feeling pressure
- Networking Strategy: A proven stealth approach which gets results
- Website Strategy: The 1 thing that you CANNOT leave off a website
- The power of Videos
- And much more

Within 30 days you can be off and running with a low cost marketing plan that takes
some effort, but little money and it will work for a lifetime. Guaranteed!

About the Author: Small Business Marketing Expert, Dr. Chris A. Hawn is an author
and online entrepreneur. He is a consultant and frequent contributor to
RBraintrust.com. If you want to jump-start your small business, attract the right
clients and generate more referrals then, contact Dr. Chris A. Hawn today. He can be
reached at chris@chrishawn.com.

When you send an article via email, you need to give them a summaary of the article in the first three lines of that email......Have the main article as an attachment that they can come back to at a later point in time. This is different than the technique mentioned above. These mail recipients did not contribute to the article.

Also make sure that your subject line catches their attention. E.g. Zig Ziglar says....They want to know what Zig is saying. Something of value that people will click thru. This is what he said and this is how it relates to my article....

Chapter 10
Networking Basics

Know your target

THE FIRST THING about Network Marketing is to understand that this is not social hour, (unless it really is).

Networking is a controlled activity with the idea that you go for 60 minutes and attempt to get anywhere from 12- 20 business cards. You're not going there for cookies and punch. It's a matter of being in front of people who can become business or send business to you.

With that said, you must also be aware that networking is like a first date. It is not a place to try to sell. What you do first at these events is look for a clear "Target Market". Here are a couple items to go over before we break it all down.

+ Be very efficient with your time.

+ Control the conversations by asking questions.

+ Ask qualifying questions so that your prospect can get what they want out of meeting you and realize the benefits you have to offer.

+ When this happens, everyone wins.

What you're looking for in your networking strategy is CONTROL. You want to go into a networking strategy with a definite strategy and an EXPECTATION. And that expectation will lead you to results.

Your plan will involve spending 3 – 5 minutes per person. Look at this network opportunity as a "1st date". Begin to build a relationship based on trust and likability. You are not there to get married. You're just looking for prospective wives and husbands. You want to qualify them, but how? Ask questions.

The ability to focus to get the information you want is by controlling the conversation by asking questions. Keep asking the person about themselves. Most people like to talk about themselves.

If you've met this person before or you already know something about them, an alternative comment might be. "I'd like to know more about what you do" This shows a bit more interest and allows them the opportunity to speak.

Try..*So what's new and exciting in your life these days?*

And when they reply back asking what you do, the easiest thing to say would be your defining statement or you could reply with something like the following.

Part of my life or what I am about is focusing on helping others. Is there anything you need or that I can do to help you?

You're going to get in front of your target market. It's NOT by going to meetings like Le Tip, BNI, Leads, or the Chamber of Commerce mixer. It's going to be where your target is, like Provisors or more focused target sites. This will allow you to budget your time. Anybody and everybody who has a pulse is not really who you are looking for. You want a Targeted Market.

Find a way to help people and show them your value. For example. You're at a networking meeting and a woman stands up to introduce herself and says "HI, I'm Patty McKinney and I work with senior women and have a boutique located at city center.

What woman wants to admit to being a senior? No one!

Try stating "I work with women who want to look good and feel great". I think all women could identify with that. Now you might add to your short intro by stating the following:

> I have a boutique located at the corner of Pine and Oak. Here is a coupon/card that's good for $5 off your first purchase. Come down to the store and sign up for our monthly giveaway where we offer a $75 spending spree once per month to the winner of our monthly drawing.

What do you do if you run in to an old friend or someone you frequently meet and see at network meetings? You can say.

> "Hey Stan, great to see you! You know why I'm here; I know why you're here. Let's talk later when we're not networking.
>
> Brief greeting only. Don't waste your network time.

Some people you may have disqualified as a prospect may cling on to you and make it difficult to get away.

Getaway Moves:

One of the first things to think about and be aware of is your time. So try these moves.

Ask a question:

- ✦ Did you get anything to eat yet?

- ✦ Walk over say excuse me; I want to talk to Richard for a minute.

- ✦ I know you want to meet others as do I. Can I call you later in the day, next week etc?

- ✦ I've got something I really want to share with you. Can I touch base with you in a few days? (The thing you might want to share is an article you have written that you think the person might be interested in).

- ✦ Use a cup of coffee or beverage as an excuse. Either get a cup or if you already have one, tell them you are going to get a heater

Once again, you are taking control of the process and you're getting yourself thru the process by once again....asking questions.

Light touch of the persons arm or shoulder and say it was so nice to see you again you; I look forward to yada, yada, yada

The getaways are endless. Create your own and "use them". After all, you're working.

NETWORKING STRATEGY

While at a networking meeting, when you find some who has given you a "buy" or "Interest" signal in what you do, tell them to go to your website to respond to your call to action. This might be an audio, video or even a coupon to download. Whatever it takes to get them to sign up for whatever you want them to. When they download the article, they will also have the option to receive future articles and material on marketing, building a business or whatever particular feature you may have identified where you can connect with them. But remember, you have given them your card with your website address and email on it.

Here's what happens

- ✦ They go to the site, put their email in, and they instantly get a page that says a link was sent to their email where they can download my promotion instantly.

- ✦ Now I have their email and they are in my auto responder list.

- ✦ Maybe use a video or audio to deliver a couple examples or presentations as well.

Look at groups such as Provisors and how these people can be referrers as opposed to clients. A bold follow up call to someone you met could go something like this:

Hi Bob, the reason I am calling is because I really didn't learn much about you at the meeting and I wanted to learn more about what you do so I can help send you business.

Keep in mind that although everyone you talk to has the potential to be a client, only a few, if any will actually need or want your services. The one thing that the majority of the people you meet will have is: Friends, family, colleagues, and employees and even people they know who are out of work. Therefore you must always consider everyone a potential contributor to your success. THEY can send you business and expand your sphere of influence. This mindset (the way you treat people in the group) will definitely bring you more clients in time. These people are a renewable resource.

Get the people you meet in the networking meeting to talk to you away from the meeting. Then engage them by asking questions about them. And direct those questions toward trying to learn more about his/her business so you can see and identify where you will be able to help them or have them use your product or service.

E.g. Call up a contact from Provisors or any other network group you belong to and invite them to get together to see how you can help them in their business and where they might also be able to help you in your business.

Giving and referring business to the other business people in your community or sphere of influence is like having them write a psychological IOW to you. That person who you referred to is going to know that you are the referrer and whether you want to believe it or not, they subconsciously know they owe you one. So keep referring and watch the momentum grow over time.

As mentioned previously, you must have a website as people will ask you about it and if you state that you do not have one, it could be a bad reflection on you as a viable business. People go where people go and people want to be surrounded by winners. Winners are up to speed on technology and the current state of business. It doesn't have to be difficult. Get a website.

Even if you work for someone else's company and you are listed on their site and in their directory, you should still create your own website/blog to facilitate your own identity for promotions, activities and events that are created by you and not your company. An insurance agent working for a big agency or association is an example of this.

Here is another example of what can happen at a network meeting.

Remember, the first step is to get the prospect to answer "YES" to a question. E.g. if you were a marketing professional you might say "Would you be interested in learning 8 marketing strategies that you can personalize that will allow you to dominate your competition"? If they say yes to this, then this is considered a buying signal and you might say "hey, would you like to set up a 5 - 10 minute meeting where I can show you how to attract the right prospects for your business"?

If you're a doctor or nutritional expert, you would say. "I'd be happy to set up a 10-15 minute complimentary consultation with you to discuss your condition and I can give you some feedback on the steps you can take on your own.

Real Estate professional: If you're at a point where you and your family are considering either buying or selling a home, I have a targeted list for (this is where you personalize it to the persons wants and needs)

+ First time homeowners

+ Foreclosures

+ Bank short sells

+ Investment properties with a positive cash flow

Or   I have a special report explaining:

+ The top 10 things you must know BEFORE you make an offer.

+ The #1 mistake buyers make when having their realtor submit an offer on their behalf. The agents don't want you to bother with this.

Get the idea?

If you haven't seen a buying signal from them you might say, can I send you an article I send to my clients that shows (whatever you have in your arsenal that is going to interest this individual?) I send these once every 30 days.

Anybody and everybody who has a pulse is NOT really who we are looking for. WE want a targeted market. This is one of the ways to find one.

Chapter 11
Cold Calling

It's not so cold

Gatekeepers:

Try to take a piece out of your defining statement to massage and make playable for this exercise; E.g. Let's say you need to get to John Jones. He is your target.

Hello, my name is Nicole Stevens and I am calling John Jones. I understand that he has a specialty in ladies footwear and is considered one of the best designers in town. Get the idea?

Or open up with…..Nicole Stevens for John Jones! When the gatekeeper says "what this is in regards to?" I'm an attorney in Orange County and I am calling you about a referral.

They may say "will he know what this is about" you can reply with. "He may not recall but I'd like to talk to him to explain what I am looking for."

I'm looking for someone who has/can a specialty and experience in patents and your name came across my desk this morning. Then make it work for YOU!

Regarding the item coming across your desk this morning. I know if I personally heard that, I would want to know more about what that "item" was that came across the desk was.

Where were THEY hearing about me? Tell them your staff/help/etc was doing the task of finding/researching this person/business and they presented you with a list. Perhaps three names were on it, if it is appropriate. You are not lying because if you looked up this person/business in the yellow pages or googled a specific keyword, they could come up and that's exactly what you did.

If you are called out as a salesman/product rep/recruiter/etc and they say. "Are you a salesman/product rep/recruiter/etc?"

Answer with a statement like: How do you mean that? Their vision of a salesman/product rep/recruiter/etc may not be what you are and it can give you a chance to explain how you are different and why they need to get to know you.

The bottom line is that you be flexible and create a more personalized approach based on who you are calling. Once you've figured out what you're comfortable with, you'll use it over and over again. You don't have to keep reinventing your line. Find one or two that work for you and stick to them.

Chapter 12
Presentations / Speaking

Aka Showtime!

FIRST OF ALL, is this something you are willing to do? How do you like presenting or speaking? Consider Toastmasters to get comfortable. I waited years before actually going to a Toastmaster's meeting. It was one of the best things I have done but the unfortunate side of it is that I waited my whole career BEFORE I went and I really missed out on some golden opportunities. The fellow members are there to help, teach and support you. They are just like you and they want to help you get comfortable and become a better speaker.

There are two parts of the speaking strategy

The first part is:

+ **The Presentation**

> **Opening:** Typically a defining question
>
> **Body:** Stories that are comprised of blood sweat and tears. Stories need to relate to the audience
>
> **Conclusion:** Has to have a "call to action" to bring the audience to you. We'll offer concepts with regards to the conclusion that will bring the audience along and entice them.

✦ How to get Marketing presentations

So now you need to ask yourself... Where might I be a presenter and use the speaking strategy. Have you thought about a speaking strategy? Remember, your activity has to be fun so if it isn't fun, we need to make it fun or forget it.

You'll want to call your contact list. And that means from anyone who recognizes your name all the way to your best friends.

Action: Call 100 people you know.

You will put a presentation together on something everyone can benefit from related to your business or what you do.

Examples:

A Realtor might give a talk on the 5 key things you need to know BEFORE you call up a mortgage broker.

A Chiropractor would have a title something like this: Three simple stress free exercises you can do at work that will lower your blood pressure.

Retail Business owner: How to know if you are getting the best price that a retail shop offers by looking at a sales tag. The key to 50% off.

I think you get the idea. It has to be something that has a hook.

So now you have your topic idea and this is what you will offer to the 100 people you know. You might be saying to yourself. I can't do this or I don't know 100 people". Remember, the people who do the little things are the successful ones. Don't wait for your ship to come in, swim out to it. You have to be hungry for success and want it. It all comes down to how bad you want it.

Here we go.....

Hi, my name is Donna McGee. We met at the Newport Beach Chamber of Commerce Mixer last Wednesday. Then schmooze but never more than 30 to 60 seconds of chit chat. *The reason for my call is that I have a question and a favor.*

The question is: Who do you know who needs a speaker/presenter for a club or organization?

And the favor is: Can you introduce me?   Note; we are not going to make a cold call.

BIG TIP: When considering the quality of the referral or connection being made from another individual, who is answering your question with; "Yes, I know this guy that works at ABC Co who would be good for you to talk to".

You have to put the referring source into perspective and ask this question.

"On a scale of I − 10, how well do you know this person?" If it is a I − 3, I wouldn't waste my energy going after this person. The relationship with your referrer is not developed enough with the referee. The REFERREE needs to have a 5, 6, or 7 rating at a minimum to be cold called by you, the stranger.

But…Instead of just blowing off this referrer and not letting him help you with this I − 3 referee, just ask him/her if they would make a call to or contact that person in advance on your behalf to see if they would accept your call.

If they say YES, you might add, Great! I'll call you in a couple days to follow up if that's ok with you. If you say this, you must do what you say and follow up with that person. Not doing what you say you are going to do is one of the worse traits you could have and you do not want to be identified that way.

Explain to your referrer that you would not want to be rude and just call someone who was not expecting the call. Then say to the referrer:

"If you are able to contact them and they said it was fine to call them, may I use your name to remind them that you are the referring source?"

Our goal here is to get you to go out in public and give presentations so that your contacts can see where you are and what you are about. You are looking for potential clients AND people who can refer to you.

Nicole Stevens, who is an attorney recruiter for large law firms, wants to become a speaker at law schools. This will not only improve her credentials, but give her increased credibility with the attorneys she communicates with. Her strategy is to get the name and introduction of the contact person for the individual school she wishes to speak at. Nicole will contact this person about presenting her program.

Challenge: Nicole will need to approach the members of the clubs, organizations and alliances she already knows and belongs to. This might even be past clients. She wants to find out where they went to law school. With a lead she can contact the right person via an introduction and make her presentation.

Another way to look at this is by using the WARM Calling technique

Doing Warm Calls

If for example you are making calls (to anyone who knows you excluding family) and out of 10 calls, you are not getting at least 2 hits, you are doing something wrong. You should be getting at least two minimum but it could be as high as 8 out of 10.

Let me take you through the processes I am talking about specifically. Take a look at the script I gave you in the section under Speaking. The following works like a charm.

Hi Jon, this is Christian Gerard. We met at the Chamber of Commerce mixer the other day. The reason for my call is that I wanted to ask you a question and a favor.

So the question is "who do you know that….?"

When using this approach, I guarantee that you will get at least 2 favorable hits out of every 10 calls you make or you are saying something wrong. That's 2 in 10 minimum. If you get zero out of 10. Stop! Re-evaluate how you are presenting yourself and begin another day. If you are getting

6 or 7, you are rocking and you better ride it while you're hot!

So I am giving you a system that guarantees that if you make 10 telephone calls to 10 people you know, you'll get at least 2 positive responses.

And don't even think about using email to contact these people and ask this question or have a staff person do it. YOU have to do it. How bad do you want to attract more prospects and generate more referrals? Output is directly related to Input.

ACCREDITATION COURSES

Believe it or not, you could present a talk to these groups. It's worth considering. One of our clients went to a financial services seminar and taught "How to Network" to the class. They got credit for their relicensing. He wasn't a finance guy and didn't pretend to be one but he put together a seminar based on the schools criteria for how to do what he taught.

Consider this. Because you put that course together based on the schools accreditation, it will be spot on for later if you do get the opportunity to present for accreditation. So if someone asks if what you teach is an accredited course, you have everything in place to say YES.

Jonathan sold medical equipment. He was able to make his presentation at a relicensing seminar that fell under the classification of technique training of which 4 hours of the doctors time in class was to be used. Not only did he get to present directly to his targeted audience, he had follow up with the interested attendees and made a few sales. You can do that too with whatever you sell or promote. It's a matter of getting to the right person and asking if they would like a presenter. What a great way to get leads.

I think by now you are getting the idea of how being able to present can really help your bottom line.

Our goal here is to get you to go out and give presentations so that your contacts can see where you are and what you're about. You are looking for potential clients and people who can refer to you.

Sample Opening:

When presenting, whatever thought, product, or action you want to leave your audience with, it needs to be the second thing you say in your introduction.

> Good Morning Mr. President, fellow members and invited guests. My name is Chris Hawn and I have a website called rbraintrust.com where we work with people who want to attract the right prospects and generate more referrals. We design and develop Targeted Marketing Strategies which will allow them to dominate their market. We guarantee that our system will bring you more prospects and more referrals than you've ever had before. I am going to give you an overview this morning of what we call our Success MAPS and at the end of my presentation, as a gift for Gary allowing me to be here this morning; I am going to offer to "arrange a 30 minute, no obligation consultation where you'll learn about our #1 Rated Strategy in building your business along with a more detailed outline of our Success Marketing Strategies."

When you make this offer again at the end, make sure you give them a call to action with contact information such as a phone number, an email address or offer them to hand you their card at the end where you will then contact them. The worst thing that can happen is NOTHING.

HOW THE PROS DO IT...WHEN GIVING A PRESENTATION

Thank the person who introduced you, dignitaries visiting guest etc. Then before you begin, try to tie in and acknowledge with humor if appropriate, something that has been said or that you have noticed in your environment.

Ronald Reagan always began each speech with TWO confirmations that everyone in the room or audience had to agree to. He did this to put them at ease and in agreement with him.

"He could be in Iowa and open up his talk saying something like

"Today on this beautiful sunny afternoon we are in the heartland of the greatest country in the world. What better place is there to have a 4th of July celebration and BBQ than right here in Des Moines Iowa?" (If you lived in Des Moines Iowa at the time, you would agree with him)

Gerry Rose, who was one of my mentors, would open with something like this:

I'd have to admit that we are all in this beautiful hotel here in sunny Southern California and the weather is about as perfect as we could ask for.

Affirmation #1: We are in a beautiful hotel

Affirmation # 2: We are here in Southern California and the weather is perfect

Gerry would now go on with his presentation.

By a show of hands. *How many people here in the room want to attract the right prospects and generate more referrals?* (Use whatever your defining statement dictates)

Please raise your hand.

Great! I'm in the right room.

Tell me. How many people here want to give their clients or customers more of what they want (in the way of customers, clients, products or sales), so that you can get more of what you want in the form of (referrals, money, time). Let me see a show of hands.

You're in the right place today!

Chapter 13
Website

The #1 thing you must have

WHAT WE DO here is create value and more often than not we want to drive people to go to our website. Initially we started out telling you that you'll take a proactive approach to passive marketing, that's where this comes from.

You must have a "Call to Action" aka an "offer of value" on your website. Use one of your articles on how to do this or do that or an e-book where you can offer a free chapter. If it applies, do a coupon.

> **Example:** Let's say we are interacting at a networking meeting. I get the sense that you are interested in my product or service but not ready to buy or commit.

I'll say something like *"John, is it alright if I send you a complimentary copy of our latest e-book.*

+ *100 Tips to getting more business or*

+ *100 ways to attract the right prospects and generate referrals or*

+ *The number 1 Critical mistake people make when trimming their trees or*

✦ *How to develop your defining statement*

You must have an Opt-in box on your website or landing page:

Here's why

Every person that initiates the download you've invited them to go to should be followed up on personally to reconnect and you can use the following excuse for the follow up. Ask them this question.

When you see that person the next time or talk to them over the phone you ask them if they received the material you offered them. If yes, ask them if they learned anything on the site about "you" or your product they didn't already know or wanted to comment on. This helps personalize things and they may very well tell you things like "I saw you were married, have two daughters, liked to travel and that you practiced chiropractic for over 29 years. This would be effective in building that relationship.

NEVER send them the e-book directly. We want them to go to our site and download the material. This requires an action step on their part. If they have even the slightest curiosity or interest, they will download the media. When they do, they are now on our list with their permission. If they don't download it, nothing is lost on our end. They're probably not a real potential client or customer and not a good use of your time anymore. We say our famous word. NEXT !

So I want to be very clear in describing this. When the potential contact is downloading, they are taking action. It is vital for them to have to take action and go to the website to retrieve the information.

Review the Steps and options

They give you their email and you automatically plug it into your autoresponder to start the process of capture. Or you can direct this person to a link on your own site (or landing page) and have them find it on their own.	This autoresponder sends them an email asking for permission to send information. When they reply, the material (article, coupon or book) is sent to them directly and then they are put into the email machine if you have one set up. This is great for subsequent follow up.

The e-book or article you write will have links within it to refer back to your website for more information or other relative articles and will have hyperlinks in the body of the media. You now have them on your list for ongoing mailings. One article or e-book can give you miles of marketing power if you know how to use it.

Some clients for example, our attorney recruiter (Nicole) may want to have two separate squeeze pages. One for law Firms and another one for candidates. Or you may want to sell product number 1 or product number 2. It doesn't matter. The party's initial review of your material or landing page is different, but from there they are taken to the same end place, your website or blog.

The books, articles and tips are instrumental in the process for giving these away for credibility, trust and confidence to do business with you.

Most people that receive our e-book or articles don't stumble upon them. They went to the site with a purpose and were more than likely driven there through one of the strategies outlined in this book. Ask yourself. Is this how the author got you to this point?

WEBSITE STRATEGY

There has to be a plan to develop a relationship with the customer that comes to your website. When they visit your site, through your material, they will see who you have worked with. Theywill also have the ability to see any other important information you may provide, and those are the kinds of things that people want to see.

Here is another place where an e-book could come into play.

On your website you have a spot or call to action that has them "click here" to read a chapter of your latest book. They sign up, you receive their email, you've been given permission to send them articles and information, and then you set them up on what I like to call, "THE MACHINE" This is where you have a series of emails that hit this person on a regular basis to establish the relationship. This technique requires that you are constantly giving quality information or tools that are a benefit to the recipient. And of course, they should be free. Have it be a teleseminar, webinar, article or whatever.

You could even ask for them to go to a spot you control where they comment on what you have given them such as an article. As a way of thanking them for this feedback, they earn another chapter of the book. Heck, you could send them the next chapter after the comment that follows that as well.

Chapter 14

Biz Expo Strategy

RODUCE A 2 ft x 4 ft sign/banner that has your logo or product picture at the top and it has a first prize, second prize, and 3rd prize. These can be produced by most print shops. I like Vistaprint.com.

Sponsored by: **STEALTH MARKETING LLC**

90 Days to Dominate your market

1ST PRIZE	*90 day "One on One" coaching and training	Value $5000
2ND PRIZE	**30 day "Group" coaching and training	Value $2500
3RD PRIZE	90 minute Personal consultation "Strategy Session"	Value $500

* Equals Ten(10) 90 minute sessions over 90 days

** Equals Four (4) 90 minute sessions over 30 days

I also have certificates potential participants can fill out to drop into a bowl for a drawing.

While at the expo or special event you want to maximize the opportunity to connect with the people. Some people and business' give something away. e.g. chiropractors give free exams, free massages, dentists offer toothbrushes and floss and x-rays, financial planners give away dinners or a free portfolio review. You must give away something of value so that when the event is over, you can do a follow up with a **"Hey you won"**. You were at the business expo last week and you won the opportunity to have a one hour portfolio review and consultation worth $500. When would you like to get together? I have time slots open on Monday and a couple on Wednesday.

Fish Bowl for Drawing

When the expo is over you have a bunch of names that you can take the next step with. It is usually quite obvious which ones actually have no interest. You never really know for sure so do the right thing, offer it legitimately but try not to waste your time with obvious "lookie loos." Remember: Time is Money.

Take your product, call them up and say CONGRATULATIONS! YOU WON!

Offer them some type of product, percentage off, or consolation to move one step closer to building the relationship.

This concludes the eight major steps to the Success System. Although not exclusive, they are the key for everything else to fall into place. There are many other ways to market your business or product but over time, many of your customers will become your good friends and having nurtured the relationships over the past many years will only make those relationships more precious. It's up to you to nurture the relationship. By staying in a person's subconscious mind by being consistent with your marketing efforts, your name will be triggered when it's time for a new referral. They will think of you.

Actions in the Advocate strategy and the Correspondent Strategy are all follow-up strategies. The strategies like the Networking, Speaking and the Business Expo strategies are what we call "pressing the flesh". Coming in contact with people.

At close inspection, you'll see that there are actually more than eight strategies included in the Success MAPS System. The eight strategies listed are the core or should I say the bread and butter. The other strategies listed in the Success MAPS are the "Tools for the Top Dog" and "Secret Weapons" which are more advanced and taught through the tutorials at various other websites including www.rbraintrust.com.

***The time it will take for you to complete this task will depend on how quick you learn to set up the basic strategies such as the list (I time function), and learn how to upload your articles, defining statement, promotions, etc. Once you have this done, you will not have to set it up again. Just upload the new material and you will be able to add on new tools and techniques with ease.

Chapter 15

Keeping Score

ERE'S A VERY important key that will help you unlock the door to your success. It comes down to time management. I know you've heard it before every way from Sunday, but it's really important and can accelerate your momentum in a way that you could never have imagined. Read the following section and do it for 30 days using what you've learned in the prior chapters, I guarantee you'll be glad you did. It really works. I utilized this process to write this book and was done in 30 days with the first draft.

Accountability STRATEGY

Some people say this was life changing for them

What this consists of is an AM (morning) question and a PM (evening) question

> **The AM question:** What High Value Activities (HVA) will I do today to realize my optimistic number?

> **The PM question:** What three HVAs did I do today to realize my optimistic number?

What is a high value activity and what is an optimistic number?

Let's talk about the **HVA** first. The HVA stands for **H**igh **V**alue **A**ctivity

Anything that will directly bring a check to your bottom line and has to do with the Success Marketing MAPS is a **HVA**. It is also anything that has to do with your rest, relaxation and rejuvenation. Remember, it must be FUN! Everything needs to be fun.

What is my **Optimistic Number**?

The **Optimistic number** is based on what we call our SRO and it is the monthly amount of money you need to reach your financial goal.

We have what we call an SRO Formula

S Stands for survival = what you need "financially" on a monthly basis to be able to survive (paying the rent or mortgage, utilities, food etc.)

R Realistic Number = (2) times the (S) number

O optimistic = (4) times the (S) number

HVA Action

When you wake up in the morning, get up and state out loud your "Defining Statement".

✦ Ask yourself to declare 3 tasks that you will accomplish today.

✦ Before you go to bed, score yourself for the day?

✦ Did I accomplish those 3 things today?

SCORE IT!

When you grade yourself each day as to whether you accomplished your HVAs, you will tell yourself that you have done your best whether you did all three or not. Part of this process is that you are going to score this every day. It's about accountability.

How many out of three did I accomplish today? 3/3, 2/3, 1/3 ?

What would you say if you scored the following by completing your externally verbalized HVA?

If you scored ...You'd Say

3/3	great
2/3	great
1/3	great

Why would I say "Great" everyday?

Every day is a great day and here is why. It's in the **RECOGNITION** you give yourself because you can do more tomorrow. If one of the tasks for the day is for you to take your laundry in or get some household item done, those are not HVAs, but you still had to do it. That's OK.

Another thing is that there are no carryovers from one day to the next. You just start over and have another great day. What we mean by that is this. If you complete five tasks that day because you were really productive, and you had listed only three, you do not get to carry over the extra two to the next day.

On the flip side of that coin is that when you only complete one task that day, you do not get penalized the next day and have to do an extra two.

Caution! Just because you don't carry over good or bad, don't let up. This has to be done for 30 days in order for it to become a habit and bear fruit.

If you are a list maker this should be good because you can just scratch off 3 items every day. This is where the real power is and it can change your life. You can go to www.rbraintrust.com/HVA and download a sample to use.

When you do this for 30 days and score it, I promise you, it will change your life. You must score it on the 3 point scale. 3/3, 2/3. 1/3,...with all days being great and that there is no carry over. As you do this for 30 days you will never look at time the same way again and time wasters will go away.

Use whatever chart you like and works for you.

An example of something that could be a time waster is a Leads or Le-tip meeting that has not borne any significant business or contacts within the last few weeks or even months. In many cases, these groups do not bring business.

You could be there for weeks and not get a lead. But to be fair about assessing this club or group you need to ask yourself if you gave to the group yourself. Did you develop good contacts and did you work a plan on how to filter out who was a qualified target? If you did not do these things, and use the techniques described in this book, then you really have not worked it at all.

WEEKLY REPORT

Daily HVA Action Plan

Massive Action = Massive Results

	Pts.	Major Objectives	Notes
M			
M			
M			
T			
T			
T			
W			
W			
W			
TH			
TH			
TH			
F			
F			
F			
S			
S			
S			

Evaluate how long you've been attending these meetings and write down how many referrals and sources you've acquired by continuing to go to these week after week. You may be wasting your time. If you're actually receiving referrals and business from this or any source like it and it appears to be cost and time effective, then I would recommend that you consider staying.

Other than that, to stay in a club to protect the spot you think someone else will take so they too can sit there week after week with no business or referrals is silly. Why are you doing this? Quit wasting your time.

Re-evaluate the people you've met. Go to lunch with them away from the group and ask what you can do for them.Learn who they are and what they are about. What are their needs and wants?

Write down the names of three people you have met that you can contact and suggest having lunch or coffee with them. Call them up; tell them you want to meet with them to get to know more about them and their business. You want to inevitably find out how you can help them. Do it now! Write down those names.

TIME = ROI   (Time = Return on Investment)

As you do this, you will see success and meet your optimistic number each and every month so long as you stay with this AM/PM HVA system.

You will make this number because you know what you need to do each month to meet your optimistic number.

Now what you need to do is create a matrix where you can check and evaluate yourself during the first 10 days of every month to see and review what you've have been doing and make adjustments to improve it.

We have a client named Randy who is in the cabinet business. His networking strategy is what he refers to as his Troika strategy. This is where he has made contacts at various events, mixers, luncheons or association meetings just to name a few. He uses the Success MAPS to follow up with these contacts to see (ARE YOU READY FOR THIS) how he can help them by better understanding what their needs and wants are.

He is building relationships first, business second. Over time he can measure where his business is coming from and based on the number of troikas (meeting with three individuals) he goes to, he can tell how many contracts/presentations/referrals he should get on an ongoing basis if he continues to do the same activities he has in the past. This is developed over time. So it all comes back to knowing where your business comes from so that your time investment gives you your best ROI. You can't expect positive results if you don't measure your results. If something you are doing is not bringing results, you need to change it or quit it altogether and replace it with something else.

NAME TAG

You must create a Name Tag for meetings, greetings, presentations and networking events.

Have a large name tag ready to go at any instance. I say large so that the people you mix with and others around you will look at your name tag to see who you are and what you do. By having your name large, they will see what you want them to see first but then the smaller logo or your short identifying slogan may get them to ask you what it's about.

Chapter 16

Business Card Strategy

They are not all alike

IRST THINGS FIRST. The overall population is getting older and with age comes poor eyesight. I know this first hand. The font size of your cards in the way of email address, phone number and address must be large and easy to read. You don't want to lose a call from a customer because they could not read your number. I'm telling you that this has happened to me on more than one occasion and I just threw the card down and said "forget it".

When you give out your business card, how many cards would you say that you give out in a 30 day period of time?

Let's say that you're giving out 12 cards in a one week period. There is a process you should use when giving out the business cards.

Step 1

Let's say you are passing out 12 cards and we discover that every time you do so, 3 people give a positive response to you for whatever your offer or offer of value is.

Step 2

Three Positive Card responses (showed an interest or buy signal)

Step 3

Two of those three people who took the card actually came and followed up for the free massage, consultation, coupon, special report or whatever your offer was.

Step 4

Whatever your conversion rate is. (This means however successful you are at closing a deal or making the sale when you have the customer or client eye to eye). Three out of five, seven out of 10, etc. Let's say that you usually close 50% of clients you get a meeting with face to face. In this case, you would get one new client because your conversion rate was 50%. That's one out of two.

In the case noted above:

We started off with 12 cards, we reduced this in the example to three, so from Step1 to Step 3 we're down to two potential client/customers and then Step 4 is whatever the conversion rate is to close the deal, purchase, signup or whatever.

It typically turns out that there are 4 steps to conversion in most businesses with most of these processes covered and identified in the Success Marketing MAPS.

Another example

You could go to a chamber of commerce mixer and meet 12 people and collect 12 business cards. So the first thing you would ask them would be related to your Defining Statement. If you get a yes and a positive signal, they may say something like "Kevin, I was looking to meet someone just like you. Can we get together? Or, can you help me figure this out? Or, what do you think about XYZ. Be ready to set that appointment right then and there while the prospect is HOT!

So let's say that you get only <u>one with a buying</u> signal. Let's say out of the 12 people you meet in that networking hour you get some people that answer YES to your Defining Statement question but they're a little bit hesitant. Maybe you get <u>three of those</u> and <u>eight people</u> are there for the burgers and dogs. So we get eight "NOs" from this group.

What we want is conversion. So in the 1st step of 12, we got four yes's of what we want. (I want a minimum of at least a warm interest) That's 33%, one in three.

So now in this particular activity, you can say that out of the four things you do a month, this one activity, in effect gets a 33% return on that particular activity. Can you see that if just one activity gets you a 33% return, then by doing more activities; you can't help but increase your production. The key once again is to focus and spend your time on "targeted markets and prospects".

Chapter 17

Review

L ET'S REVIEW WHERE we have gone so far in understanding the critical first eight steps in implementing the Success MAPS.

Step 1

Create your defining statement.

Step 2

Communication Strategy

While reaching deep within yourself or your business to find your defining statement, you will have to tie this in with how you or your business communicates with the outside world.

Evaluate your website. Is it current? Does it reflect current technology and is it easy to navigate? Most importantly, does it have a call to action?

Are your email addresses professional or are you still bob @aol? The way you communicate is very important and when someone who I am about to do business with or work alongside has an email that is not tied to their business name or some other personalization, I assume in the back of my mind that they are not on the ball. This could be wrong and is just an opinion (and I know everyone has an opinion) but I believe it to be true. At least I can say that this is the way my staff and I have always looked at this perspective.

Are your business cards professional? There is absolutely no reason not to have a professional business card. They are so cheap to obtain at (www. vistaprint.com) there is no excuse.

Step 3

Advocate Strategy

The advocate strategy consists of 25 people that bring the world to you. You must never ask them for anything. Only communicate to them with things of value. You can send them books, articles, and cards at the holidays or something personal that means something to them.

So find 25 people that you can either train to send business to you or that you can naturally have business sent to you. Treat them like the Golden Goose.

Step 4

Correspondent Strategy

This is all about staying in touch with your larger audience on an ongoing basis. You can write an article every 30 days and send it out to a number of people like your friends, colleagues and acquaintances or even patients. And you have to remember to do it with permission if you are utilizing email. Go back to the section on networking where it describes techniques to get permission.

You also need to be very good about removing a person from your list if they request it. Respect the individual.

The articles need to be something that you are passionate about. If it is an article, it needs be from 500 to 700 words, contain a bio at the end and a direction to your website or blog. This aspect of using an article or video overlaps with our advanced strategies.

Step 5

Networking Events

You need to set a goal of attending at least 4 network events every 30 days. This could be Chamber of Commerce events, BNI meetings, Provisors meetings, Troicas, or just have coffee or lunch with someone who is in business or a new acquaintance. Perhaps a new business owner in town who really doesn't know anybody yet. Go welcome the person and introduce yourself. You're going to call these contacts up for a lunch or coffee to get to know them better and learn about their business.

If you don't make a conscious effort to meet this goal, it puts a kink in the chain of the "Success Marketing MAPS"

Every 30 days go to these events and collect cards of the people you meet. This is where you utilize that article or website strategy as described in a previous chapter. You may have a competitor who does something really well and gets a lot of business because of it. I can tell you with great certainty that if you combine all these tools and strategies together your competition won't have a chance against you. After all, you've now read the book and are ready to get the ball rolling. You'll be impossible to stop.

One thing I want to encourage you to do is find ways to communicate with people other than calling them up and saying "I'm just calling to follow up" That is a turn-off unless there was really something that you had to follow up on. Do some research and make your follow up connect with something your target can identify with.

Step 6

Speaking/Presentations

Once every 30 days you need to speak to a group that is in your target market. The speaking strategy is very simple and it works if you will just do it. Remember what I said about Toastmasters. Check it out today. Google toastmasters for your geographic area.

As an example but certainly not typical is that a colleague of ours received 48 engagements to speak as a result of this speaking strategy. That's almost one per week for a year.

The way he did it was that he called his contact list and did two simple things. He called up anyone and everyone (not related) he knew in his database relative to the geographic location where he provided his business (insurance). He asked them just two questions:

1. Do you know anyone who is looking for a presenter for their club or organization?

2. Can you introduce me? (You're looking for someone to make a connection)

Review the chapter on Speaking.

You need to find folks who will connect for you and the way to do that is to ask. The next three strategies are things you need to do every six months.

Step 7

Website/Blogsite Strategy

The website/blogsite involves our videos, audios, e-books and articles. Remember that they are created only once and you will get miles out of them. They don't have to be long.

You want to make your book somehow tied into your defining statement. So it is critical that you identify things that you can create once and use over and over.

You'll find that almost everyone you offer your e-book to via a download, also goes through your website. There they can find out a lot more about you or your product and service. Let me ask you a question.

Did you look through the website/blog before you got to this spot in this book? You see. It's easy. We all interact that way. We're curious, we want to learn more. You can do this just like I have. Just follow the Blueprint.

When you looked at the BIO, did you see how you can share with fellow marketers in your bio where you might share that you are married, involved in your community, do philanthropic work, or are a member of Rotary?

For them to personalize you helps build credibility and trust. Afterall, the reason you do all the networking you do is about building relationships. Business and money come down the road, after you've earned it.

After you build credibility by building a nice website or blog that has something attached to it of value, you should be good to go. You only had to do the website once. Just for those naysayers out there. Yes, we will have to revisit the website periodically in the future for updates and maintenance. But not rebuild it from scratch. The blogsite is a living form. You can add to it regularly with new posts, videos and a whole gamut of tools to add content. I strongly suggest you do so.

A website is like a brochure where you can describe your business, your products and services. It does not have a life of its own like a blog does. Someone has to know how to get to your website by having the URL or from a link elsewhere.

The blog lives on the internet and can be constantly changing by your added content, comments and opinions. This of course drives traffic which is a book for another time. There are plenty of sources out there to learn the intricacies of driving traffic to your site. Billboards, magazines, and newsprint have their place but they are constantly shrinking and are losing their cost effectiveness as compared to the target the same dollars can reach through the internet. There is just no comparison.

So if you plan on staying in business, you have to get a website and preferably, also a blogsite.

Step 8

Business Expo

This strategy can work for many applications.

+ You hold a raffle or give out a prize

✦ The person has to sign up to be able to win

✦ You collect the emails and names for a follow up

Sample Realtors

At one of your open houses you can offer the raffle. As a first prize you offer something of quality value. E.g. closing costs for that client, an iPod or pay for the appraisal.

Advertise it, publicize it. Do it maybe one time per year.

What will happen is that people will want to sign your book and give you that contact information.

Some people who are looking for a home will not want to make a connection with the realtor for various reasons. They do not want eye contact. They just want to go through the house and move on. That's OK, You collect their contact information.

The prizes that you give out can be varied but you want to be able to say "Congratulations" or "You Won" or "You're the Winner"

So now at least when you make that contact someone wants to hear what you have to say.

The Last Thing

One last thing, I want to encourage you to write a book.

Using the right people you'll be able to fine tune your ideas, get help with editing, production and distribution. You'll get great feedback from friends, family and colleagues. It will truly come together.

With today's technology it's easier than ever to write and publish your own book. For fractions of what it used to cost. You can write it in 30 - 60 minute increments on an ongoing basis until you are finished. That is exactly the strategy I used to write this book.

By doing it in small increments, you remain fresh and revitalized each time you sit down to write. It's OK to stop and say "that's it for today or tonight". You need to give yourself permission to walk away when it begins to feel like work. Just stay the course.

Parting Wisdom

There is a famous quote that says:

"Don't wait for your ship to come in. Swim out to it."

I'd like to think that you swam out to your ship when you bought this book. You now have your hands on the wheel and you are the Captain. Make the most of it by steering true and straight ahead…Destination Success!

Some great sites to check out when writing a book:

Lulu.com--Blurb.com --Createspace.com--Fastpencil.com

Or just Google the term "self publishing"

About the Author

Author, chiropractor and 21st Century marketing expert Dr. Chris Hawn invites you to take the eight steps necessary to put your system into action and dominate your competition. Dr. Hawn is a consultant and frequent contributor to RBraintrust.com. If you want to jump-start your small business, attract the right clients and generate more referrals contact Dr. Chris Hawn today. He can be reached at chris@ChrisHawn.com.

Chris, as he likes to be called has been a chiropractor and marketer for over 30 years. He attended and graduated with honors from the prestigious Palmer College of Chiropractic in Davenport Iowa. Since graduating in 1981 Chris has started and opened three successful clinics in Southern California.

Throughout his life, Chris has been committed to community service and promoting good will throughout the city of Dana Point California where he resides. He was a charter member of the Monarch Beach Sunrise Rotary Club when it formed back in 1988 and has been working in service with Rotarians for the past 22 years. He met his wife Terry in one of the early meetings and they have been married for over 20 years.

Traveling the world and seeing how other people get it done has always fascinated Chris as he has spent most of his leisure time traveling around the globe. Australia, Tonga, Ecuador, Panama, Mexico, Indonesia, Southeast Asia, Thailand, Laos, Cambodia, Europe, Ireland, Norway and many more.

Chris and his wife Terry have spent most of their free time volunteering and providing support as members of the Dana Point 5th Marine Regiment Support Group www.**danapoint5thmarines**.com. Early on in his career, Chris heard the king of inspiration Zig Ziglar speak and talk about "getting wired to be inspired". This is one of his many mantras as he works to become wired to get inspired just as Zig does everyday of his life.

http://www.Chrishawn.com

Notes

Notes

Notes

www.ingramcontent.com/pod-product-compliance
Lightning Source LLC
Chambersburg PA
CBHW071237170526
45165CB00003B/1136